FLOURISH

HOW TO START, FUND, AND GROW YOUR BUSINESS

TERRY LUKER

FLOURISH
— How to start, fund, and grow your business

Copyright © 2020 Terry Luker

Published by BookRipple
www.BookRipple.com

ISBN: 978-1-943157-98-3
Printed in the United States of America

To reach the author, go to:
www.ACStn.net

Dedication

This book is for every entrepreneur out there who wants to flourish and is:

- Hungry for more than average
- Passionate to fill the "gaps" they see
- Chomping at the bit for more
- Courageous enough to start a new journey
- Willing to take risks to fulfill their dreams
- Wanting to launch their own business
- Done with a mediocre lifestyle

If this rings true for you, then you have a partner to help you along the way!

That is my aim. It's time for you to flourish!

— Terry Luker

Table of Contents

PART IV: BUILD YOUR TEAM

PART V: PRESS ON

PART VI: FLOURISH STORIES

Introduction

I love the deal making process and I am passionate about putting those deals together for the entrepreneurs behind small businesses across the country. I am not as passionate about big business, though it has its place and needs in our society.

You see, small business owners really do drive America. They are what built America. Sure, politicians talk about it all the time, but few have ever sweat over meeting a payroll obligation or worried about the health and well-being of their employees, the people who depend on that small business owner for the job they have and the livelihood it creates for their families.

Most people believe if they want to start a business they need to get their bank's blessing so the bank will loan them the money. The problem with that is most banks are not interested in financing a new start up business without some type of guarantee that the new business will succeed.

There are several programs that are available for business owners and prospective business owners. One such program is SBA Lending and is part of the Small Business Administration (SBA). Over 99% of all banks in America today claim they offer SBA lending.

The SBA is where banks can have the guarantee they are looking for. The SBA provides anywhere from a 75% to a 90% guarantee to the bank for the business loan – so the bank is on the hook for only 10-25% of the loan if the loan defaults.

Unfortunately, most banks today have no clue how to handle small business lending. I recently met with a prospective client who had been waiting six months for a local bank to approve and fund his small business loan through the SBA. The bank finally came back and told him his loan was declined by the SBA. Later we discovered his loan was never even submitted to the SBA!

Regrettably, that is what many banks do to small business owners. When that owner applies for a loan at their bank – *you know, the same bank they have had their payroll account and their operating account at for years* – the bank drags out the process, sometimes for months, before telling the business owner that they simply couldn't get the loan through the "committee" or that the SBA wouldn't approve their loan. (Keep in mind that the SBA doesn't actually fund the loan, they simply guarantee a portion of the bank's loan.)

So, what can a small business owner do?

I have always had a fondness or passion for finance. Over my 20 years in the automobile industry, I acted as more of a CFO than a salesman. Now don't get me wrong, I am first a salesman and proud of it, but selling doesn't start until someone says "no." If there are no objections, then you either did a great job covering all possible objections or you've become an order taker and have not provided salesmanship.

In my career in the automotive industry, I have been tasked with renegotiating bank loans for dealerships, getting home mortgages for the owners and senior staff, acquiring commercial real estate loans for the growth of our business, building and designing new buildings for our companies, ensuring the flow process was correct, and negotiating better deals for merchant services.

Most dealerships have "floor plans" that provide funding for the cars you see on each lot. The "floor plan" has an expense to it and that is also a negotiable item. Believe it or not, many automotive dealership owners are not well equipped to handle banks and lenders. They often have another party handle the initial negotiations through the end of the deal, only becoming involved towards the end at the deal closing or "final table," as I like to refer to it.

So what can the small business owner do? I have a developing relationship with the Chairman of the Board for a rather large lending institution. In one of our breakfast meetings, he made this statement to me, "The federal government has basically made all banks nothing more than a utility company."

While I can't be sure if that's his original quote or a repeat of something he overheard in a meeting, when you stop to look at banks and how they have been performing since the 2008 "financial adjustment" period, you'll find they are not lending money to grow their own banking business.

Here is an interesting study for you to undertake. Go and fact check this information. Look at the amount of money banks had on deposit with the federal reserve *prior* to 2008 and then look at the amount of money that banks have on deposit with the federal reserve today. The difference is staggering!

If banks aren't making money through loans, then how do they make a profit? Banks today are making money through three ways: acquisition, investing, and fee income. Read the press clippings of any bank (they are usually exceedingly proud of their growth), then research the acquisitions they have completed that year.

Investment income comes from a bank investing its deposits in something that is a very safe investment. Many banks invest in government securities and make a profit based on the difference between their cost (such as interest paid for deposits) vs. what the security investment pays to the bank.

Fee income comes from a variety of methods, from the money banks charge us to use checking accounts to all the fees they collect for any additional services they provide. They also earn a small interest payment on their money by safely having millions of dollars on deposit with the federal reserve.

Reserves have been required by the Federal Reserve Bank (one of the places banks can borrow from) for years now to ensure that the banks have the money to cover their obligations – an insurance policy against massive bank failures. But only recently (since 2008) has the Federal Reserve allowed banks to collect an interest payment on those funds.

One prominent banker told me, "Of course we are going to put our funds on deposit with the Fed, especially if we are not making money anywhere else on those funds."

The interest banks earn on this money is only .25% but when you look at the numbers, you'll see how much this small percentage really adds up. Based on the August, 2019 Fed report (Federalreserve.gov), the amount of money required by all banks in America to have on deposit was just under 150 billion dollars. Yet the amount of money that banks had on deposit with the Fed was 1.3 trillion dollars. That amounts to deposits of over one trillion three hundred billion dollars, and they are making .25% interest on that money.

Now you see one of the reasons why the banks really are no longer in a lending mode! They would rather make money from fees and the investments they make.

So again, what can a small business owner do? Thankfully, there are still some banks that are in the lending business. The problem is that a small business owner might not know where to find those banks and might be unfortunate enough to be doing business with a bank that is content to keep their loan balances where they are.

One business owner, who is now a client of ours, recently told us he had been to 26 banks before he found one that would loan him money. This client has a net worth of over 10 million dollars and has outstanding credit. Going through the loan process 26 times, only to be rejected, cost him a lot of time, research, and focus which would have been better spent on his business operations!

I realize banks can't stay in business just making a .25% return on their money through the Federal Reserve. I do believe, however, that it gives some banks pause on offering loans to small business owners. While .25% on dead money might not make the bank profitable, it can offset expenses.

While our company, Commercial Capital BIDCO (an ACS affiliate company), makes sure we are getting paid on our funding account, that is not how we make money. It still helps to receive some type of payment on our unused funds during the month.

Until six years ago, I never realized how difficult it was for business owners to find money to grow and expand their businesses. A good friend of mine who shares a passion for finance and business told me that I had "missed my calling" and should have gone into commercial loan brokering. I never knew commercial loan brokering was even an industry. Some call it shadow banking or loan brokering, but I simply refer to what I do for a living as providing solutions.

I detest the term "loan broker," mainly because of the horror stories I have heard from clients. There are some bad brokers out there claiming they can provide money to businesses for an upfront fee. My company only has one program requiring an upfront fee and that is our bridge lending program which is funded through our affiliate company Commercial Capital BIDCO (CCB). We provide the underwriting and loan origination for CCB and must collect a due-diligence fee prior to completing the work to get the loan funded.

At my company, the business owners are issued terms for the loan prior to having to pay the due-diligence fee. If for some reason the loan is not fundable, the fee is returned minus any third-party reports that had to be paid for.

We never ask for upfront money from any clients engaging us to find funding solutions. If you are looking for someone to help you acquire funds to grow and expand your business, I recommend carefully checking out those companies and reading the fine print.

We receive calls every month from prospective clients who have already paid thousands of dollars to a "company" that they have never heard from again. One such client was a hospital group, and though we could not help them either, it didn't cost them anything to find that out.

Business owners today need an advocate in the lending arena who can help them work through their financing options to provide workable options for acquiring capital to help them meet their growth goals.

In addition, even some large businesses are finding they need outside help to find the funds needed to grow and expand. Good commercial loan specialists get paid for what they do, for the relationships they have, and for their knowledge of the lending world, and in the long run it will save most companies money.

The time requirement is prohibitive. Business owners are aware of how much time it takes to look for a lending partner, wait on banks to reply (most likely with a loan rejection), and have the correct loan package in order.

Finding money to grow and expand a business is an art that many business owners simply do not have the skillset or desire to undertake.

This issue can't be simply summarized by saying all banks are bad. What I am saying, however, is that every bank has its niche and every bank has deals they like and deals they simply will not do. There is no list of these deals on their website or in their lobby. You can spend your time trying to figure out which bank likes what type of loan … or you can engage the services of someone who already has this information and handles this process for a living.

Most business owners have a passion for what they do and skills that are unmatched by anyone around them. If they don't, they ought to sell their business!

What most business owners don't have is a network of outside advisors who can step in and help them through a growth mode or a downturn with an honest evaluation of where they currently are, where it looks like they are headed, and what the likely result will be based on the current path.

Business owners need that type of help, and the owners who will lead in their respective industries are the ones who are actively looking for those answers today.

What they need might be an interim or part time CFO (we have a virtual CFO), a business expert or business coach (we have one), an outside opinion from an outside CPA, or simply a new set of eyes and ears on their business.

To be successful in an ever-changing business world, you need access to the right suite of advisors. We can put them in front of you or you can find them by asking the right people.

Small business owners helped build America and they are still the backbone of this country … and I will do all I can to help them grow and succeed!

PART I

Do What Moves You

What is it that you want to do? That is really the first question you must ask yourself. You have got to begin there.

Next, what do you see out there that gets you fired up? What makes you say, "Yes, that's exactly what I want to do!?"

Once you have your goal figured out, then it's time to take strategic action.

Remember, when you are doing what you love to do, it's really not like work.

CHAPTER ONE

Free to Choose

I love what I do, and I am truly blessed to be able to come to work each and every day doing exactly that! Wouldn't you love to say that, too?

Years ago, when speaking with an employee who was leaving our company, I said, "What you are doing is not your passion. Even if I won the lottery and was set for life, I would be at work the next day because I am doing what I love to do."

Thankfully, each one of us is free to choose how we spend our time at work and at play.

Back when I was in the automobile industry, working mostly in the finance department, I saw firsthand how important the finance department really was. It could make or break a deal. The finance department might be the difference in a month that's a disaster or a great month. If a customer's deal could not be sold to a bank or other type lender, then nobody would make any money. That includes the sales department, the service department, and the accounting department (if there is no money, there is nothing to count).

As a direct leader, if you aren't doing your job right, I am going to make sure you are aware of it and try to help you make the necessary changes, so you can get to the next level of your career. Or I am going to help you change your career.

> Givers have to set limits because takers rarely do.

That's my approach. I recognize that many people do not do well with direct and focused leadership, but there is no excuse for poor performance.

When I have terminated employees in the past, I have had to accept that I either made a poor hiring decision or I could not find the key to unlock that individual's talent.

This way of thinking has taught me to be slow to hire. For example, when we hired our Senior Credit Officer, it took me four months to make the decision. (She has done such a great job, I won't let her leave!)

Some people have told me that I am too trusting of people, but I have always believed that given the opportunity, people will do the right thing. Sometimes I am right and sometimes it just doesn't work out that way.

Call me naïve or "old school" or worse, I have always had a desire to see people succeed in life, to be all they aspire to be in life and to accomplish more than they ever dreamed they could accomplish. Someone has to believe in them, right? Many people over the years have believed in me.

During those 20 years in the automobile industry, I helped a lot of people create and expand successful careers. There are also many people I should have cut ties with long before I eventually did.

Again, I'm still learning.

When I was leaving my last car dealership position, I was naturally considering my future, trying to figure out what I truly wanted to do. I liked the financial side of business, but what I was doing was not exactly my dream job.

At that moment, a seemingly insignificant opportunity arose. It was 6 a.m. on a Saturday morning and I discovered that the University of Alabama football team was staying just 40 minutes from our home. I had known they were going to play Texas A&M later that day, but I had no idea the team was staying so close.

> Change is not a threat, it's an opportunity.
> – Seth Godin

(Don't quit reading just because you're not a fan of Alabama football or Coach Nick Saban. Hang on so you can get my point!)

Not always being a spur-of-the-moment guy, that morning I grabbed my youngest son and drove over to catch a glimpse of the team. When we arrived, we were greeted by several grad assistants who informed us that we could not speak to the team or coaches and that they would not sign autographs as it was a game day.

We discovered the policy that greeting fans and signing autographs only happened on the nights before a game, but my then 11-year-old son was with me and we didn't want to leave quite yet. The grad assistants pointed to a hallway where the team activities would be in and said, "If you just sit there and don't bother anyone, you can watch."

We did just that. For three hours we watched a perfectly well-oiled machine. Everyone seemed to know exactly what was supposed to happen and they executed it perfectly. We saw Coach Saban step into the hallway on several occasions to take calls from a phone that an assistant coach would hand him.

It was an amazing sight to see. No wasted movement or time. Everyone made the meeting they were supposed to be in, everyone was on time, and the whole "process" seemed to run smoothly.

As we sat there, a nice lady (who turned out to be the aunt of one of Bama's best players) started talking to my son. When her nephew, a star player, came down the hall to board the bus for the game, she made sure that he met my son and took a picture with him. She made our fun day extra special.

> Caps we put on ourselves are the ones that limit us the most.
> –John C Maxwell

On the way home, I realized I had seen exactly what I wanted! I knew I would never be able to be a part of a mediocre organization again. I wanted what Coach Saban had developed ("processed" is what Alabama fans call it). I wanted a first-class organization where everyone knew what to do, when to do it, and was proud to be a part of the team. If it was less than great, then I had no desire to be a part of it.

A new reality was taking shape in my mind that I could finally put into words:

> If you don't ultimately own it or have absolute control of it, you will never make something all that you want it to be.

Whatever I did, I wanted it to be great. I wanted it to be smooth and well-oiled. I wanted, through it, to be able to provide great value, while showing kindness and respect to everyone. I wanted it to be real. And above all, I wanted it to work, to be profitable, and to win.

I would have to own it and control it, which meant it had to be mine.

That morning the idea for my company was born. I knew I was good at making deals that involved financing. I also knew that I wanted to help people realize their dreams. That was about it, but it was enough to start with.

I did not know exactly what my company would become, much less have a name for it (the name Alternative Cash Solutions came later from my former partner, Ken Collins, during a cold week of training in Albany, NY), but the germ of an idea had taken root! The name changed in January of

2016 to Alternative Capital Solutions to reflect more of what we really do.

Zig Ziglar was someone I have admired all my life. At one point I probably owned or at least had listened to everything he had ever written or recorded. My sales teams probably grew tired of his sayings and his wisdom, but I never did. One of the things Zig said was that if you help enough people get what they want in life, it will push you to get what you want in life. I believe and live with that philosophy in front of me every single day.

So, I jumped in and worked to create a company that would be all that I wanted it to be … and that leads me to the purpose of this book, which is:

> To help prospective business owners gain the knowledge and insight to start, fund, grow, and expand their own businesses.

I want to help you realize your dream and live a passionate life. I believe a truly fulfilling life is one where work is fun and exciting and where the goal for a balanced life of family, friends, and business can be met. My hope is to help you see that you can achieve all your dreams if you are willing to put in the work.

So, let's begin!

PART II

Chart Your Own Path

After you have sorted, clarified, and found what moves you (what you are *truly* passionate about), it is time to learn all you can about how to turn your passion into a money-making, income-supporting business.

The first step is to search out the very best leaders in your field and try to learn from them. You don't have time to reinvent the wheel, and the great news is that you don't have to. If you want to be competitive or lead in your respective industry, you must first learn your industry inside and out. One great way to do this is by finding a mentor who is an expert in your field of interest.

You will face a learning curve, that is a given, but there is no reason why you can't make your learning curve as fast as possible! If you truly love something, learning about it won't be a chore.

If you are like me, I learn from talking with people and hearing about their experiences. Listen for all the information and not just for what you want to hear. Too many times we have conversations and we only hear what we want to hear and not what is truly being said.

Also, if anyone tells you that starting their own business was easy and that they had no barriers to overcome ... they are not being honest with you! Listen between the lines and you will figure out if what they are saying really adds up. Maybe they are soft-selling the process they went through. Or maybe they are even trying to sell you their business!

As my grandmother used to say, "God gave us two ears and one mouth for a reason." That's still great advice, especially when it comes to learning about the industry that interests you.

CHAPTER TWO

Be Mentored

Can you get into a mentoring relationship with someone in your chosen field who is willing to work with you? Or maybe there is a mentoring program in your chosen field or industry? Local civic organizations may be a great source to find these types of programs. You have to look for them, as no one is going to lay them at your feet.

I remember asking one individual to mentor me and he looked at me like I was crazy. Then he informed me that he was mentoring his wife. The look on his face was of disdain, as if saying, "Why in the world would I want to mentor you?"

Though I could have taken offense at his response, the reality was that he did not want to mentor anyone, much less work with someone who was not part of his own tight little circle. What's more, his reply opened my eyes to the fact that I thought way too highly of his organization. My mistake, but I learned!

I also learned that I needed to develop a relationship with someone before asking them to mentor me. Many people claim they want to help grow those around them, but few really mean that. It is an unfortunate truth about people.

After a bit more studying, I realized the person I asked to mentor me had poor leaders in key positions of his organization. Why? Because he didn't know how to grow his people. He didn't even seem to understand why growing people was important to a successful organization!

Quite frankly, he was all about the money and not about growing a great team. Here is the fact of the matter:

> Great organizations grow great teams and they are not afraid to spend the time and the resources to do so.

There are plenty of people out there who are never going to give back to anyone, much less share what they have learned.

Thankfully, my request to be mentored was declined!

Perhaps you have dreamed of working with someone. Maybe you even asked to be mentored and were turned down. Don't be offended if the door slams in your face. Instead, be thankful! And remember not to mirror their behaviors once you build your successful organization.

> Great organizations invest in their people so they can build great teams.

You can find great people in any field or any line of work who will mentor you, you just have to know where to look. I have found a lot of great leaders in local civic organizations, which is why I recommend them. Many of these leaders are approachable and some may be willing to share insights of what worked and didn't work for them. Even if you can't establish a mentoring relationship, just listening to them will teach you a lot.

The key point to remember is that this is something you have to initiate. You must make the effort and be willing to meet on their terms and to fit into their schedule for this to work.

Trust me when I say it is extremely frustrating for a leader to offer his/her expertise and then have to wait 5 or 10 minutes every time they meet with you. That is a sure way to get the boot, not to mention ruining any chances for training within your desired industry.

Treat a mentor with respect, be humble, look to learn, and you will be amazed at how things turn out in your favor!

Course correct if needed

When you chart a course to anywhere, getting even slightly off track can be a big deal. A mere one degree in miscalculation can send your ship to an entirely different country!

If you ever saw *The Profit* TV show, you watched as Marcus Lemonis, a brilliant businessman, would take what he knows and turn companies around and get them making money again. What an incredible skill!

Any business will fare better if it begins the correct way. And if that fails to happen, the odds of that business succeeding are greatly reduced. I have seen countless business owners, who started without knowing the proper steps to grow and expand their business, end up off course and eventually went into bankruptcy.

The secret is to get on the right course and then stay the course. No doubt that will mean minor course corrections here and there, but you can do it when you know where you are going.

That is another excellent reason to have a mentor by your side. It is all part of charting a path to your success!

Remember, great mentors are not there to just be a cheerleader; they are there to ask you tough questions and make you think (and even re-think) the direction of your company.

Do not get hung up on the "mentor" term. We have a business coach who has been with us for several years and he is a "mentor" to us. I never make a major business decision without running it past him for his thoughts and comments. His name is Joe Martin and he is what I call a "business guru." He knew nothing about our business when he began working with us, but what he did know was to ask questions and to listen to ALL our team members' response to his questions.

He has been a great asset in helping my oldest son and I learn to really work together. He was also instrumental in teaching me that if I wanted to build a great organization (like I said I wanted), then I had to learn to delegate the work and let our team do the work themselves.

Surrounding yourself with great people is paramount to success in your business and in all areas of life.

CHAPTER THREE

Do Research

Researching your field of business is imperative, especially if you cannot find a mentor or do not have the time for such a relationship. Utilizing research instead of a mentorship is a much tougher approach, but it can be done. Either way, research is good to do, but much of what you learn through research could be accomplished through a mentoring relationship.

When I speak of research, I immediately think of a paralegal. Attorneys ask paralegals to investigate something or someone and paralegals return with pages and pages of information.

Before I meet new clients, I like to know something about them. Any background information can be useful. There are great tools these days to help, such as LinkedIn, Facebook, blogs, and other public information.

What I'm most interested in is knowing about their accomplishments. Do we have common ground that could break the ice in our first meeting? Or do they say things or post pictures that are contrary to who they say they are?

Real research, however, is much deeper than browsing social media. Digging deep means finding out if their company or operation does things the best way possible and understanding why.

That means you must learn the strengths and weaknesses of the industry.

What are the strengths?

When you are looking for what your industry strengths are, it's also important to find out *why* those things are strengths.

You need to find out:

- What has caused those things to be considered strengths of your selected industry?
- How long has this been a major factor in your industry?
- What is the likelihood that this industry will continue to hold those strengths?
- Is it a seasonal industry or does it look like it has a long shelf life?
- Does it appear to have a lasting use and what is the previous history of the industry?
- What are some of the things that could or will have an economic impact on the industry?
- What is the benefit to the customers?
- Is the benefit to the customers easy for them to replace?

These are deep questions that, when answered, will shed incredible light on what you are pursuing.

Here is an example that may help with the reasoning and logic behind such an approach:

SportClips:

If you are familiar with SportClips, you know it to be a great place to get a reasonably-priced haircut. It's a boys' and men's haircutting establishment. (I've had my hair cut at numerous SportClips locations.)

Strength – *employee satisfaction*: One of their strengths appears to be employee satisfaction. I always ask the employee cutting my hair how long they have been cutting hair, how long they have been with SportClips, and what they plan to do. Several of the employees I spoke with had once owned their own salon, and yet now they work for SportClips … and love it! That says a lot for a company.

Strength – *long shelf life*: Another strength of SportClips is that people need haircuts in good times and in bad. In an economic downturn, there might not be as many MVP cuts (including steam towel with shoulder and neck massage), but there will still be a lot of regular haircuts. That is the sign of a business with a very long shelf life.

As you dig deep to find the strengths of your desired profession, you may uncover unexpected opportunities. When I began to research the need for ACS, I never realized how badly business owners and prospective business owners needed someone to help guide them in financing or refinancing their businesses.

I uncovered great opportunity when I learned the competition claimed to help companies through the financing/refinancing process, yet most of them did not actually follow through on their commitments. What a great opportunity to shine!

> Never interrupt your enemy when he is making a mistake.
> – Napoleon Bonaparte

I also discovered that many companies in my industry tried to disguise themselves as an actual "lender" when in fact they had no money to lend.

What's more, I found that many companies charge an upfront fee to prospective clients, whether they ended up helping them or not.

An obvious business opportunity was staring me in the face:

> If we provide great customer service, if we are honest in what we can and cannot do, and if we only get paid when we provide funding, we will have more business than we ever imagined.

This reality has proven to be true.

Most likely, that same reality will hit you square in the face as well! As you do your research, I would bet that several obvious opportunities will jump out at you.

Why existing companies didn't provide basic services was beyond me, but what it meant was that there was plenty of room for me to excel. And in your industry, I would bet you can uncover the exact same thing!

What are the weaknesses?

Too many times in business we focus only on the things that we like to look at. This positive-side-only perspective can be dangerous when it comes to researching a business. Don't fall for it.

You need to weigh the negatives because this is how you get an accurate picture of what you are looking at. The fact is, every industry has strengths (or they would be out of business) and every industry has weaknesses (or it would be too good to be true).

Choosing to ignore obvious weaknesses just because you love the industry is a recipe for disaster.

Let's look at SportClips again:

> **Weakness – *employee turnover*:** One potential weakness was that their model required a lot of people with experience in cutting hair. Who is going to manage all those employees in all those stores? And how will you keep them?

This is certainly a potential weakness, but from what I've seen, SportClips does a great job of handling employee turnover. Finding and keeping great hair stylists and barbers could be a weakness, but they have found a way to address that very real issue.

Weakness – *finding new employees*: Where do they find new, qualified employees? That's always a challenge for every business, but what was their secret? I asked around and found one store owner who got his new employees from local beauty schools. He established a great relationship with the schools and they in turn liked being able to offer employment opportunities to their graduates. A potential weakness of SportClips turned out to be a win-win.

Weakness – *pushy selling*: One weakness that I have not seen remedied at SportClips is the constant overselling of their products. Maybe they have a strong commission program on all product sales because they are going to try to sell you their products every time you come in. I personally don't like this approach, but others may not mind it.

Whatever weaknesses or perceived weaknesses you uncover, be honest and address them for what they are. Don't hide them or pretend they don't exist. If you discover a weakness in your proposed industry, go investigate it further. Find out why it's a weakness. Maybe it really isn't.

If you know your tendency is to bury your head in the sand, thinking a weakness won't be a weakness if you don't look at it, then I challenge you to get an honest opinion from another person who will tell you the truth. Commit to addressing the issue, for that will prove growth on your part.

> It's not how much you do, but the effectiveness of what you do that counts!
> –David Byrd & Mark Smith

Now comes the good part! After you have thoroughly researched the weaknesses, what opportunities do you see? How can you turn a weakness into an advantage? What is a weakness that could bring you greater growth?

I applied this same process to my ACS company. In my research on weaknesses in my industry, I found that banks today have loan portfolios that are falling. However, they really don't have much control over falling loan portfolios because they have become so regulated by the federal government. The banks have so much regulation and so many agencies overseeing them, they simply cannot please everyone.

You would think banks would combat their declining loan portfolios by going out there and looking for new business, right? Just the opposite is happening, which is a sign of more weakness!

Banks will decline a loan simply because the applicant is not an existing client of the bank. That in its simplest form is discrimination, yet nobody seems to care.

I decided their loss would be my gain!

To prove my point about the banks and their many weaknesses, here is a good example. Not long ago, we at ACS had a client with a very high net worth. Much of it was in liquid assets (cash and cash equivalents). The local bank informed me that they were not interested in doing a deal with this seemingly ideal client … because the bank was saving that space in their portfolio for only their current clients!

The client had $15,000,000 of actual cash on deposit with several banks and was willing to move those funds to this particular bank, but the bank didn't want the business!

> Resist change and die, adapt to change and survive, create change and thrive.
> – Ray Noorda

Banks depend on your deposited funds to run the daily operations of the bank. That means your deposits are one of the main sources that banks use to fund new loans. Banks can borrow up to 10 to 1 basis of their capital. Depending on who you ask, outstanding loans are an asset to banks and can affect their capital and therefore their ability to borrow more funds against their capital.

Turning down a client with that much cash seemed like a really bad business move, and it was all because he wasn't a current client! I would have liked to have read the bank's letter to the client declining his loan request!

What are you going to do about it?

Weaknesses can be overcome with great planning, location selection, area of operations, and people. Above all, hiring the right people is the best way to overcome weaknesses, but we will discuss that in greater detail later.

Identifying the weaknesses in your prospective business will go a long way in building your business plan and getting your business off the ground quickly. This will also prove to lenders, investors, and creditors that you have completed your homework.

When you are dating someone, do you just look at all the good and ignore any problem areas? Eventually, everything is going to come into the light, whether good or bad, so it's important to pay attention early on. Similarly, in business it pays to know all the strengths and weaknesses up front, or else problems will "unexpectedly" arise.

It is smart to keep both eyes open and to objectively address all the facts.

Once you have done your research and/or completed your time with your mentor, you should have a pretty clear list of all the strengths and weaknesses of your prospective company or business.

At this point, you need to honestly determine if you still have the same passion and desire to build this business.

Do you? Are you still passionate about it?

If so, then it is time to figure out just how to make money doing what you love and how much it is going to cost to get started. This is where the prep work really starts to pay off!

CHAPTER FOUR

Network

Networking will be one of the most valuable tools at your disposal while you contemplate building your business and will become even more valuable to you once your business is up and running.

I moved to middle Tennessee in late 2013. I knew no one in the business community when I moved to the Franklin/Nashville area. I just knew that it was centrally located and would make it easier to get around the country as opposed to Houston, Texas where I had lived for over 18 years.

How do you build a business when you don't know anyone in the industry your business is tied to? I did what I like to call "doing it the old fashion way." I began by cold calling bankers and commercial lenders and taking them out for food or coffee. In the first three years of our company, I would say I paid for over 200 such meetings.

My message was very simple. I explained to them what our company did and how I could help them increase their business.

To those in lending institutions, I explained that if they had customers they wanted to keep in the bank, but could not approve their loan, they could send them to me and I would fund their loan request with an out-of-market lender. This was an ideal solution, as it met the customer's loan needs and allowed the bank to keep the deposit relationship with the customer.

Despite the win-win message, it usually fell on deaf ears, because (as I knew) most bankers are not truly interested in helping their customer if their bank is not providing the funds. There were several exceptions to this, and those exceptions became the people I built relationships with.

Out of those 200 meetings, about one-third generated business for me. You may think that is a terrible return on my investment and time, but we are still in business! And I still get calls from some of those 200 people today, which leads to direct business for our firm.

Additionally, another important thing I did during my 200 meetings was asking questions of those bankers. I wanted to learn about their bank and the way they did business. This would help me in the future to know if deals I had that needed funding were a good fit for these banks or not.

Networking is how you build your business. Everywhere I go and in everything I do, I am always looking for the potential to discuss our business and what we do for clients. For me, like the old American Express "Don't leave home without it" commercial, I never go anywhere without my business cards.

I am not pushy about our company, but over the years I have developed the ability to be patient and simply plant a few seeds here and there in a conversation. This makes whoever I am talking to end up asking me questions about what I do for a living, and then it's game on!

Naturally, not every person I meet has a need for a commercial lending solution, but every person I meet knows someone who might need our firm's services.

The other part of networking is for your own growth. You are meeting people who can help you when you get stuck in your business. For example:

- Where do you find the best attorney to help you in your business startup?
- Who has the best CPA firm?
- Which local publicity agency can best help you with getting the word out about your new business?
- What about the best printer to use for business cards and your other printing needs?

Networking always provides you with different options and opinions, and that will in turn open additional new relationships for you. Some will be great leads, others not so much.

One sure way to be successful at networking is to never eat lunch alone. Try to have some type of business meeting or meet with someone you want to get to know. Make your lunch as productive as possible.

I have found that most people enjoy helping other people. Network as widely as you can. You never know when one of those meetings or people is going to open the door to a great business opportunity.

You will also need to network to fill some of the internal gaps you will have in your new business, especially with local hiring. There is no way you can hire all the full-time help you need right at the beginning, but there is no need for you to do that. We will talk more about this later.

PART III

Get What You Need

Armed with a clear vision, and a course mapped out as thoroughly as possible, the next step is to obtain the elements necessary to launch your new business.

They say luck is what happens when preparation meets opportunity. It's not really luck then, now is it?

This is all part of the preparation for your success.

CHAPTER FIVE

You Need:
A Great Business Plan

Of all the things you will need, the first step is a great business plan. A business plan is exactly that:

> **Business plan:** A plan that you have for your business to begin operations and that sets certain measurements to determine your progress. It will include a pro-forma of the expected performance of your business as well as cash flow charts to show when your business can expect to be cash-flow positive.

Over the years, countless businesses have failed to even get off the ground because they could not raise the capital they needed, all because of a poorly-prepared business plan.

Learning how to put your business plan together, correctly can be the difference between success and failure.

For example, a relatively new company came to us recently to see if we could help them repair their cash flow. They had received terrible advice originally and had crafted a business plan that left them short $100,000 for all the equipment and operating capital they still needed.

Two different banks had given them loans (through their SBA 7a program), but sadly the company asked for our help when they were only one step ahead of the debt collectors. There was no time to implement a new financing plan and the company had to file for bankruptcy protection.

This company didn't know it when they opened their doors, but the fact that they were short $100,000 from the start meant the owners were soon forced to leverage their personal credit cards and scrape money together in an attempt to simply survive the initial cash-flow crunch. They could have survived, and perhaps even thrived, had they planned better, but by the time they realized their error, the banks were not willing to help.

When they met with us, they had acquired four different high-cost merchant cash advances totaling $85,000, and their payment on that debt was $11,000 per month! The company was in a no-win situation. This payment on the debt destroyed all their cash flow. They simply couldn't swim that fast upstream!

Is there a better answer to such a tough situation? Absolutely! With a properly-prepared business plan, the two SBA loans could have easily been structured to

> When achievers fail, they see it as a momentary event, not a lifelong epidemic.
> – John C. Maxwell

include the additional $100,000 for equipment and operating capital. Spreading that note out over 10 years would have provided ample time to create successful cash flow for the company.

Due to their poorly-prepared business plan, the owners were forced into bankruptcy, putting property that had been in their family for years at risk. Instead of having a thriving and growing business, they were faced with the possibility of losing everything they had.

I can't stress it enough ... you must have a great business plan and it must be thorough.

The elements of a great business plan

The many parts of a great business plan are less daunting when you think of it as making a great sandwich with the bread on the outside and the slices of cheese, meat, and veggies on the inside. It is doable!

We are not talking about creating a rocket bound for the moon! If you are thinking, "I'm not sure I can do this business plan thing," rest assured, you *can* do it.

> **Element #1 – *Provide a summary:*** Your business plan will need to include a brief

summary of what the business actually *is* and what it *does*.

Element #2 – *List competition:* It will need to identify who the competition is and where they are located.

Element #3 – *Show opportunity:* One of the biggest pieces of your business plan needs to be the clarification of the opportunity you see. Why is there an opportunity for your business to be successful? Also, define what your market area will be.

Element #4 – *Explain operations and roles:* You will need to very directly describe how you will operate the company and what the key roles of people in the company will be.

Element #5 – *Outline costs:* In your business plan, you will need to identify all the startup costs that you will incur while you are getting the company up and running. This will include pre-launch, opening, post-launch, and the daily running of the business. That includes everything from the cost of forming your company, to the facilities you will operate from, to the payroll you will need until the company starts to generate its own income.

Element #6 – *Include operating capital:* You will need to include all operating capital you need until your company is cash-flow positive. To put it simply, you need enough operating capital to keep the company afloat until the company can afford to pay its bills with the cash flow being generated. This is vastly important to many phases of getting a company off the ground and running, and a lender (if you are borrowing money) will not even consider your loan request unless your business plan includes this.

I suggest that you read these elements again. You will see that they are doable, especially if you tackle them one at a time.

Dissecting your business plan

When you submit your business plan to a lender, it feels like you are on the operating table surrounded by doctors with scalpels. Though that may seem true, take a deep breath and press forward.

What the lenders will do (with their scalpels) is to take the pro-forma out of your business plan and dissect it. They are going to underwrite their loan proposal based on their own stress test that they have in place for new startup businesses.

Many people will tell you that you cannot get a loan for a startup company, but that is simply not true.

We have helped many startups get the funding they needed, but no lender will give you a dime if you fail to come to the table with a great business plan.

What exactly is a pro-forma? Though it may sound a little daunting to some people, it is actually very practical.

Pro-forma: A spreadsheet normally done in Excel format that outlines the first five years of a business's proposed operations, listing all the realistic expected income and all the expected debt (with a category for miscellaneous debt).

When you add the income and debt expectations up, the business plan will show the total money you should expect to need to open and run your business until it gets to the positive cash-flow point in your pro-forma.

Based on your own well-researched statistics, the lender should be able to see your expected financial future.

A pro-forma will normally need to have the first three years completely itemized and broken out on a monthly basis, while the last two years can be shown as a yearly summary.

It is completely normal for companies to take several months to a few years before their cash flow is sufficient enough to cover their debt.

Preparing your business plan

There are a lot of companies who can help you prepare a quality business plan. There are several companies we will recommend to you.

But whoever you use, the preparation of a business plan is not free. What's more, the burden of gathering all the information and putting it all together falls on you. Others can help, but nobody can write the business plan for you.

That is what you, the entrepreneur, get to do. It is both your duty, as well as your honor.

Two words of advice:

> #1 – Don't be so stubborn as to not take great advice.

> #2 – Don't be so easily swayed away from what you know to be true.

Keep going until you have a really great business plan.

If you have completed your homework, done your due diligence, identified the strengths and the weaknesses of the field you want to compete in, and listed all the associated costs to start the company, then you have a clear plan in your head. That's perfect!

> Your business plan will determine to a large extent the success or failure of obtaining funding.

If you have been working on your pro-forma and you now realize what the costs are going to be to start your company, you are in a powerful position. You see very clearly where you are and where you are going. It's exciting!

Press through the process.

Sadly, many people never get past this point. For some reason, they freeze up and don't get this far.

A final word of advice:

Keep going!

CHAPTER SIX

You Need:
A Good Resume

In addition to your business plan, you need a good resume. A resume, at its core, is really a "proof" document. It's all about whether you have what it takes to run your business.

After all, anyone (equity investors, venture capitalists, banks, or private investment funds) investing in your business wants to know that the business has a greater chance of success than it does of failure. What you show in your resume is just that – proof that you can bring about success.

> **Potential weakness –** *You lack experience:* If your resume does not reflect your ability to do what your new company aims to do,

that's not good, but it's not the end of the deal.

No, don't fake it! Rather, identify who is going to run operations (because that person does have the experience) and provide their resume along with yours.

For example, I had a doctor client who wanted to open a few restaurants. He made a great income, had great credit, and had money to put into the deal, but he had no experience in running a restaurant. His resume said he was a waiter during college, but that did not qualify him to run a restaurant.

> Your attitude determines your altitude and the balance in your bank account.

We found someone who had experience to run the restaurant instead of him. That resume took care of the "experience" question. Then we completed the funding information to open the businesses and his funding was approved. Today he has two locations up and running!

People start new careers in industries they have a passion for all the time, but very seldom do people have a true passion for something they have never been involved in before.

Yes, the doctor opened restaurants, but someone else was tasked to run them, daily. Sure, he could have quit his present job, given up his medical license, and purchased his own restaurant, but that would have been much harder, slower, and more expensive. He would have been reinventing the wheel in many areas, and that is almost always a waste of time (and money).

Usually, what we do in our work or free time prepares us for a "parallel industry" or "parallel path." That is much more common, and from the perspective of investors, it is also a much safer bet.

Creating your resume

If you are not familiar with preparing a resume, simply sit down and write out every job you have ever had, including internships and volunteer work. Write it all down.

Once you have it all written down, step back and look at your list. When it is in print in front of you, it is easier to see how all you have done up to this point has prepared you for where you want to go.

It makes a jump to a "parallel industry" seem very natural. The lessons you may have learned in life during an internship or working in a nonprofit as a volunteer may be the driving force in your desire to start your own company. Don't forget to list any clubs you belong to or groups you are affiliated with.

Once all your experiences are listed, and you have evaluated how they connect and what you have learned, you are then ready to put it together into a quality resume. Such a resume will have greater meaning to you and to those who are reading it.

The next step is to invest in having all the information professionally prepared. There are companies that specialize in crafting resumes.

They know what reviewers want to see, so draw on their experience.

Do what it takes to create a great resume!

CHAPTER SEVEN

You Need:
Commitment – Be All In

The difference between a successful business and one that never gets off the ground is what I call the "all in" affect.

That means you are in the game, you are committed, and you are serious. There is no room for "maybe" when it comes to building a business. The doctor client I mentioned previously was in his restaurants every single day after his office hours were completed and all day on weekends. He was committed.

Many times, when I am talking with future business owners, they will tell me they are starting their business as a part-time venture.

That is not a good idea! It is hard enough to start, build, and grow any business, let alone trying to do it on a part-time basis. Investors also don't look kindly on the part-time approach, because it usually means part-time effort.

Admittedly, many great businesses were started out of garages or as a part-time gig. I am not one of those people who could ever do that, but statistically speaking, the odds of a part-time business venture succeeding are lower than that of a full-time business venture. Usually, 100% focus, time, effort, and energy are required for business success.

It is impossible for your future company to be an industry leader if you have a part-time level of commitment.

I must admit that I am one of those people who doesn't even want to play if I can't win. It is one of my weaknesses. I have to live with the fact that nobody in my family will play Monopoly with me, as I want to own all the property and control the whole board!

For me, to be "all in" means that my company is my complete business focus. I live it, breathe it, sleep it, and am constantly thinking of how to make it better. Everywhere I go, I end up talking business.

My wife and I were standing on a corner in Times Square in New York not long ago, and two men standing nearby made a comment about my 'Bama football logo on my shirt. We ended up talking commercial lending. The upstart is, that chat may result in a meeting with their company president and CEO in a few months to discuss how my company can help them!

Commercial lending is what I do and it's what I am passionate about. I love putting deals together! The truth is, if I gave it 50% of my focus, our business would probably be 20% of what it is today!

What I do is both my passion and my hobby. I never tire of working and helping business owners grow and expand their footprint because when I am successful for them, I am growing and expanding my own business footprint.

What about you?

Be honest here: are you growing your business with an "all in" mentality or with an as-I-can-get-to-it approach?

I know of a car dealership that had a great owner/entrepreneur. He ran an excellent business. On Mondays he would come in and look at the weekend sales numbers. If it was a bad sales weekend, he would go through every detail. He would look at the appointment logs and the Up Log (the registry of every person who showed up at the dealership over the weekend). He would visit in detail with every sales manager and all his sales team, trying to find out if it was advertising that didn't work or if the team was simply not working as hard as they could have been working.

Years later, the owner/entrepreneur sold the dealership to a public company. He had to agree to stay on and keep the dealership moving forward. When he came in that next Monday morning and saw the sales numbers were down for the weekend, he told his sales managers not to worry about it. "We will get them next time," he said, but there was no passion or drive in his voice. And *that* is the difference between an owner/entrepreneur and a manger of a business.

Only you know what it really means to be "all in." You have to have a strong drive and desire to succeed in your industry or you wouldn't be here. Just promise me this:

> You are going to be "all in" and accomplish what you set out to do.

Don't settle for anything less!

CHAPTER EIGHT

You Need:
Funding

I used to watch the *Shark Tank* show on television, but I can't do it anymore. I used to cringe every time I saw entrepreneurs and business owners give away their businesses and ideas for mere peanuts!

Sure, they needed investment capital for their business, but trying to raise that capital on *Shark Tank* is a horrible way to do it. Though the phrase "giving away the farm" has been around a lot longer than that show, the show is a perfect example of what you should not be doing for your business.

If you are a business owner or a future business owner and you need funding, then you need a commercial loan specialist, not a 60-second spill-your-guts moment on national television.

I have had countless business owners come to me, after we have arranged their financing needs, and say, "I just didn't know where to turn to get the funds we needed." That is one meeting I enjoy being a part of!

Most people view local banks as the one and only source for funding. If the bank says "no" to them, then they conclude that it must really mean the answer is "no" to funding.

Thankfully, that is not the case.

Banks do not make the process easy for anyone. Truth is, most banks and lenders are scaling back to save money by putting tellers in bank branches and centralizing the lending into larger banking centers.

In the not so distant future, you are going to walk into a bank and be greeted by an oversized looking ATM machine. You will conduct all your business on that machine and if by chance you need to speak with someone from the bank, you'll simply press a button and someone from a centralized location will show up on a monitor to speak with you.

Sound crazy? It's already here! Chase Bank already has several of these locations. The end result is that it makes it almost impossible to develop a business relationship with the true decision makers in a bank.

What's more, these banks have become so specialized that you cannot deal with just one person for all your business needs. The person you speak with at the bank might specialize in

> Whether it's commercial real estate financing, commercial lines of credit, floor plan lending, equipment leasing, or help with receivables ... a good commercial lending specialist is your lifeline to the financing you need.

non-real estate loans or commercial real estate loans when you simply are looking for a loan to do some capital improvements or to buy equipment.

A commercial loan specialist, on the other hand, can save you time and money by knowing where to turn for the specific type of lending you need. Most lenders have niches or special types of lending that they like or are limited to, so knowing which lender fits which type of loan is valuable information.

Lenders often have a specific industry (i.e. the hospitality industry, such as hotels) that they enjoy working with, which could mean their portfolio is unbalanced, and may not leave them with additional funding available for their choice industry.

What do you do then if you happen to be looking for a loan to build a new hotel? Your bank loves you as a client, but their hands are tied because their "bucket" for hospitality lending is full.

Sadly, I can assure you that your banker is not going to refer you to another bank down the street! That is not going to happen. Some banks will string along the process of getting your loan completed with hopes that you will get discouraged and change your mind about building that new hotel.

Regardless of how difficult it might be to deal with your bank, you really can't blame them. You are a good client and the bank wants to hold on to good clients, but they also have regulators and boards to answer to.

But just because you cannot blame your bank does not mean you need to take their answer as gospel!

Just stop playing their game! Instead, get that second opinion. It may be the difference in your business getting off the ground or never getting started.

CHAPTER NINE

You Need:
Passion

The last thing you need to be successful in your business venture could very well be the first requirement: *passion*.

Without passion, there is no real reason to be doing what you are doing … but with passion, the sky is the limit! You know exactly what you are doing and why you are here. That is power right there!

Passion moves you to act, and that is what you must tap into.

Personally, I love the deal-making process and I am passionate about helping small business owners. My passion is for small business and the people and entrepreneurs who play such a vital role in our nation.

Seeing opportunity

When you have passion, you see things other people never see. Your heart beats to a different drum. It's as if you are tuned into a different frequency.

You envision things and you want to help make the world a better place as a result.

What does this mean on a practical level in your specific business? Quite simply, it means you can see clear and evident "gaps" that need to be filled – services that need to be provided.

Other people can't see those gaps, but you can. You are tuned in.

Usually, these gaps are also opportunities just waiting to be worked out and implemented.

For me, my passion to help small business owners, mixed with 20 plus years of helping owners deal with financial issues, has helped me identify huge problems small business owners must face daily.

> If you are not living your passion ... are you really living a fulfilling life?

The evolution to creating my current career derived from the passion I have to fix the problems I had experienced.

Small business owners are what drive this country, but until politicians have lost sleep over meeting payroll or worried about the health and well-being of their employees, there are always going to be gaps that policy makers never see or ignore. Most politicians will never understand how small business owners think, which means they have no desire to help them. They have other worries, such as getting re-elected.

Yes, as we have discussed earlier, the government has a program to help small business owners, but sadly most banks today have no clue how to do small business lending. There are gaps everywhere!

We have had many clients over the years tell us how long the banks made them wait *before* they were finally given a "no" to their loan request. They all lost time and money for having to wait unnecessarily.

I have often wondered how much closer these companies would have been to success had the banks had simply said "no" right away. They could have found the correct lender to work with a whole lot sooner, that is for sure!

The bank has their reasons for justifying their delay tactics and decisions, but small business owners are not only hurt as a result, they are left to fend for themselves in most cases.

I only know of a few bankers who actually try to help their clients find other solutions when the bank cannot help them. Imagine if every bank would simply do this!

This is one such gap that I am passionate about filling.

Isolate the problem

Once you isolate the problem (see the "gap" in your specific industry), it is time to offer a solution. It is, after all, what you are passionate about.

> Many of life's failures are people who did not realize how close they were to success when they gave up.
> – Thomas Edison

But can you really fix it? Your solution may fix a small issue, a small part of the overall problem, but it may never repair the entire issue. It's important to remember you don't have to fix everything. One solution to one problem can be enough.

In my world where I am passionate about helping the small business owners get funding, I have isolated the problem. The federal government has turned banks into nothing more than utility companies. Since 2008, banks have changed. They don't lend money like they used to. Very few banks are growing organically – that is actually growing their loan portfolios or their book of business. In other words, they are not lending money. That may not seem very much of a news flash, but it has become extremely difficult for small business owners to access capital from banks.

Offer a solution

One of the greatest assets that we offer at ACS is knowing which lending partners are looking for which type of loan. This knowledge makes all the difference in the world to small business owners.

Prior to working with any bank, we look at their loan-to-deposit ratio. This ratio defines how much of the deposits the banks have on hand have been loaned out to borrowers. The higher the ratio, the less funds the bank has available to loan out.

If a bank has a large loan-to-deposit ratio (something above 93%), we know they are not interested in lending additional funds. What's more, we know there is really nothing we can do to help those banks.

Some banks have self-imposed limits. I know one bank that has it in their charter to never be above an 80% loan-to-deposit ratio. As a direct result, any lender with these types of limits is not going to be a large player for us in the commercial lending arena.

Remember the business owner from earlier who went to 26 banks before a bank finally agreed to loan him money? You would have to agree that he lost a lot of time and money working through those 26 prospective lending partners. Imagine if he knew from the start where a bank was that would likely lend him the funds he needed. Think of all the time and money he would have saved!

> If you have a vision for it, you can accomplish it.
> – Zig Ziglar

You have your own examples and stories in your industry that make your blood boil. Those are proof that you are doing something you are truly passionate about.

When you get mad, it's a good thing. Channel all that energy and passion into your next solution!

Passion grows

Passion is like a tree that keeps growing and growing, needing more water and sunlight. Of course, a fully-grown tree gives you greater rewards (i.e. shade, fruit, etc.) than a tree that just sprouted.

Passion grows and expands, so don't be surprised if you learn and grow, then turn around and learn and grow some more!

Soon, you will find yourself doing it again and again and again.

It is all part of becoming more and seeing more, a good and natural part of growing.

On the business side of things, the growth of passion usually runs parallel to the growth of new ideas and new opportunities you have. You guessed it; this is an unending cycle of growth!

This two-fold blessing is something you can both look forward to, as well as expect.

Fakers are obvious

When you are passionate about something, it usually takes you a millisecond to spot someone who is pretending to share your passion.

They say illogical things like, "I know exactly what you mean" (you know they have no experience) or "I love your kids as much as you do" (which is impossible) or "This is the only way it will work" (they have only tried it one way).

As a solutions provider, I really try to help other people by providing them with effective solutions. This goes back to the "isolate the problem" and then "offer a solution" challenge that we have already mentioned.

This means we are not:

- trying to make people's lives more complicated
- wasting people's time
- blowing people's money
- ruining our chances for a referral

It's common sense, but fakers don't care. They are usually interested in one thing and one thing only: putting *your* money into *their* pockets.

For example, in my world of helping small business owners get loans, there are a lot of fakers. These fakers usually charge an upfront fee before they even try to get you financing. And if they are unable to, they still keep your money! Some of these companies will even take your money (usually thousands of dollars) and brazenly never call you back!

My approach is different. If we can't get you the funding that you need, then you pay nothing. That is as fair a business model as I can see.

Network to fill internal gaps

Most business owners have a passion for what they do that is unmatched by anyone else around them. That is usually just the way it is, and it is a good sign.

But for those business owners who have no passion for what they do or less passion than their competitors, they should seriously consider selling their business. Get out while the getting is good. Sell to someone who has passion. Doing so will benefit everyone.

As we've already discussed, most business owners don't have a network of outside advisors who can step in and help them through a growth mode or advise them through a downturn. Passionate business owners have the same challenge.

Regardless of the business, new needs pop up at different times. Maybe you will find yourself needing a part-time CFO, a business expert, or another opinion from an outside CPA.

You want to be successful and you are passionate about what you do, so if you see a "gap" in your

> Passion is about doing business in such a way that every job done has the potential for positive word-of-mouth marketing.

own company, network until you find someone who can help you fill that gap.

The people you need are out there. Keep asking and keep networking until you find the right like-minded people to fill your internal gaps. This is all about making you stronger.

The truly great are truly humble, and if that means finding someone to help you along the way, then do it with passion!

For me, I have found very few business owners with the time, skill set, or desire to get the funding they need to grow and expand their businesses. It's a gap they have in their business, but don't see it. As a result, their business is in a sort of pause mode, which probably hurts them more than they realize.

Always expand your network to fill any gaps you might have, and be open to those in your network exposing gaps that you might not see.

All of this is so that you can grow faster, be stronger, and do more of what you are passionate about.

PART IV

Build Your Team

As the business owner, you dictate the temperature of your company. If your team sees your passion, drive, and desire to build a great business, they will feed off that. If they see you coming in with a bad attitude due to an argument at home, they will feed off that as well.

It's hard to come into your office every single day with a great attitude, as some days life just gets you down. But trust me when I tell you that your team will immediately pick up on your attitude and mood! Your business will reflect your own choices and sunny disposition. When you walk through the doors of your company, you have to leave everything else you are carrying – the extra baggage – at the threshold. You simply must choose to be great. Attitude truly determines your altitude!

Create the culture by which everyone thrives. The culture of your company is directly driven by you. You cannot delegate that. Your team's culture will be a direct reflection of you and how you conduct yourself.

You can do it! When you walk in the door, you choose your attitude, and what you choose for the day affects your entire company.

Your staff define the company

I am very blessed and fortunate at ACS to have great people on our team. We have an awesome team. My oldest son, Jeff, runs the overall operations of our company and Micah Seadorf, our Senior Credit Officer, runs our credit team. Micah has Julie Luker, Tracey Bailey, and Alyssa Gideon on her team in the credit department. Roger Williams is a partner in developing new products and markets. Ken Collins is still somewhat involved with us, even though he keeps trying to retire on me. I depend on Ken for special projects. Each person has unique talents that combine to create a winning team!

CHAPTER TEN

Find Your People

Building a great team is about people … do your people know you care about them? There are several ways to ensure they love working for you and are dedicated employees.

This all begins at the hiring process. Do you take your time and use a consistent hiring practice or policy? Hopefully your system is more thorough than just hiring anyone who happens to come your way when you need someone.

Formerly, in the automotive industry, the only requirement to be hired on as a salesperson was to prove you were breathing. The saying was, "If they can fog a mirror, let's try them on."

Most companies (the good ones anyway!) have thankfully moved away from this "rigorous" hiring practice.

What is your approach to hiring new employees?

Have a bench

To "have a bench" means that you are always looking for new talent to add to your team. You have a bench ready for them!

For that to work, you must always be scouting and quietly looking for the next team member. Wherever you go, whenever you shop, and wherever you rub shoulders with others, keep your eyes open for talented people.

What exactly are you looking for?

Begin by:

1. paying attention to the service and treatment you get when you are out and about.

2. being observant when there is a stressful event going on in a store – see how it was handled, and more importantly, who handled it.

Watch those around you who play a part in meeting your needs. Do they do it well?

Bench system

When you have a need for new talent or find the talent, does your bench have a system? And does your team know what that consistent hiring process is?

Honestly, that is one of the biggest and brightest ways your employees will know you care about the growth of your company. When they see you take care of a new hiring need according to your system, that speaks volumes about you, your company, and those around you.

If you have such a bench system, do you always adhere to that hiring process? What about when

> Success in business requires training
> and discipline and hard work. But if
> you're not frightened by these things,
> the opportunities are just as great
> today as they ever were.
> – David Rockefeller

your son or daughter, niece or nephew, or sibling is looking for a job?

Your process should have steps that are known by everyone in your company, such as:

> *Step #1* – **Hold multiple interviews:** Each potential candidate should be interviewed several different times by several different people.

For example, not long ago I was traveling and happened to sit by a young lady who was employed by a large national firm. She had been with the company for three years and commented on how hard it was to get hired in the first place, but quickly added that it was a great company to work for once you become an employee.

I was listening! What she said spoke volumes for the company! They had a process, it worked, and she trusted it. That is the benchmark you are looking for. You want your hiring process to be hard, but once they are on the team, they love the culture you have created.

>   *Step #2 – Do background checks and employment verification:* You show you really care about your company when you know who you are hiring. An initial background check and verification of previous employment is paramount to hiring a great team. This is not only a bare minimum standard, it is a smart place to start.

You only want to interview potential candidates, so screening out the non-qualified prospects is vital. There may still be a few who get through but having a screening process in place will save you a lot of wasted time and effort, while at the same time improving your hiring odds.

Sometimes, you may even want to consider hiring an outside company to help with the screening process. If it saves you time and energy, especially during a busy growth period, it may be a smart move.

For example, when I was in the automobile industry, many dealerships would use an outside company to perform background checks. One company often used was The Cole Group. We told new prospects that we used The Cole Group to run checks and employment verification, and that alone took care of some prospective employees! They would quit filling out the application and leave. Why? Because they knew the truth of their background would be exposed through The Cole Group.

> Do or do not. There is no try.
> – Yoda

A quality prospect has nothing to hide, so weeding out the "riff raff" through a company that simply verifies employment and does a background check can really help you out.

Of course, the responsibility of making the hiring decisions rests with you, but having accurate and consistent information up until that point is vital to the success of your process.

Be consistent in the application of your hiring process. Even when you are in crisis mode, you cannot fudge when it comes to hiring. Your team is watching, so keep it your benchmark to only hire the best, and only after they have been processed.

CHAPTER ELEVEN

Build Your People

Part of finding the right people and building the right team comes down to your own desire for what you believe to be the right culture.

What are you building within your team? Do you really want to be normal? What is normal anyway?

There's a saying that we become what we spend time doing. Take a brief step back and consider the following questions. It will then help you run forward with greater clarity!

I realize the questions I am about to ask you are not ones you can directly ask in an interview. Your job as the owner/interviewer is to figure out how to get the answer to the questions you believe are important to you and your company.

One way that I do this is through the setting of our interview. My office is configured with my work station and then four chairs set up in a sitting room type of space in front of my desk. There are two soft and comfortable chairs and then there are two regular hardback chairs. The chairs all face each other.

The first thing I like to see is which chair my guests or appointments sit in. I want to put the person being interviewed at ease so we can have a conversation without them thinking it's a strict interview process. The more comfortable they are with me, the more they are going to open up about themselves, their families, and their thoughts.

My office is filled with University of Alabama memorabilia as well as family pictures. There is usually at least one conversational piece that someone coming in will be drawn to. This gets us started and then I try to simply allow the conversation to flow so I get the answers I'm looking for. This is how you can control, to an extent, the culture coming into your company.

Here are questions you need to answer:

What is normal?

#1 – Work life: How does the work life look for those who want to join your team?
- How many hours a day are they at work?
- How much of their off time are they investing in their own growth?
- How do they view their current job?
- What is the average time they spent on previous jobs?
- Do they appear to be a follower or a leader at work?

#2 – Home life: How does the home life look for those who want to join your team?
- Are they stable?
- Have they been in multiple relationships recently?
- How long have they been in their current relationship?

- How many children do they have, if any?
- How much time do they spend with their family?
- How much time do they spend with their friends?
- How much time do they spend in their community/church?
- Would they say there is "balance" in their life?

#3 – Social life: How does the social life look for those who want to join your team?

- Do they appear to have a lot of friends?
- How much time is allocated to friends?
- How much time is allocated to their belief system?
- What do they do for fun?
- How much time is allocated for fun?

#4 – Belief system: What does a normal belief system look like for those who want to join your team?

- What do they believe in?
- Do they live out what they believe in?
- Do they invest in their belief system?

#5 – General categories of normal: What is normal, in a broad perspective, for those who want to join your team?

- What does their health look like?
- What does their family look like?
- What do their friends look like?
- What are their routines?
- How are they influenced?
- What are their good/bad habits?
- What do their finances look like?
- What makes them tick?

Be better

Why all the questions about "normal"? It is to make you think, to ponder, and to clarify. What type of team are you building anyway? Only you can define what you want your company culture to look like, which means you are defining what normal is to you and your company.

Naturally, nobody wants to be "normal" if normal means being boring, status quo, a non-performer, or stuck in the mud.

But if a "normal" employee means consistent, quality, on time, and with a great attitude, I would take that type of normal every day.

For those who reject the "normal," I challenge you to really clarify what it is you want. What does the opposite of normal really look like?

Once you define what the opposite of normal looks like, then you must decide if it is something you want for your life!

> Are you willing to do whatever it takes to be a high achiever?

I believe we want to be better and to better ourselves in every area of life. That means you must choose your "normal" and then go out and make it happen.

What do highly successful people do? You want that to be "normal" for you and your team. You want to be a high achiever and you want your team to be a high achieving team as well.

Let that be your new "normal" as you strive to grow a great team, culture, and business!

CHAPTER TWELVE

Believe in Your People

Too many leaders live in fear. You see it with politicians, college professors, CEOs of publicly traded companies, and even mega-churches. The leaders live in fear of losing their job.

As a result, they quit doing what they know to be best for their constituents, students, employees, or congregations. They refuse to take on an unpopular stand, even if it's what's best. They choose not to rock the boat by embracing a new way or a new idea. They stick with policies and procedures that are harmful and damaging … so they can hang on to their job and title!

Why? The answer is simple. They are afraid. It's called fear!

Choose to believe

True belief in people is rooted in freedom. You must free yourself from fears so that you can believe in those around you. Leaders who micro-manage, steal the limelight, or discourage creativity are really bound up in their own fears.

When you are fearless, how do you act? If you were fearless, how might you act differently than you do right now?

> It pays in many ways to be flexible and to bend. Always remember that.

Living life without fear is what we all must strive toward.

Get free from fear yourself, then lead those on your team to that same freedom. This will bring the creativity and life to your company and culture that you want and need.

For me, I desire my team to be free to express themselves. Their thoughts and opinions matter to all of us, so I want them to have the freedom to disagree with me. I want them to have no fear in helping to grow our company.

To believe is to bend

If you have played with icicles in winter, you know they are brittle. There is no bend in them!

Leaders who stubbornly refuse to listen, much less change, are setting themselves up for a painful shattering. It is both inevitable as well as a huge competitive disadvantage for a company during the refuse-to-listen season. Everyone, except the leader, is probably painfully aware of the situation, but until the leader chooses (or is forced to) change, it's not going to happen.

Back when I first started to manage finance departments, I insisted that all finance managers wear a white shirt and tie or a white blouse. That was my requirement, but it admittedly sounds a little ridiculous today.

As a leader, you owe it to your team to listen to new ideas and suggestions. Letting others speak and present their creative options for growth will bond them to your team, so that is an immediate win. And if they indeed spot a "gap" that you might have missed, that brings even more benefit to your company, and you win all the more!

Be willing to bend a little. It will keep you limber! It will also help build the team culture you want and need.

Yes, change is a risk, but your job as the leader is to take risks. It comes with your title. Success demands that you be open to new ideas and to change.

> If you see a bandwagon, it's too late.
> – James Goldsmith

But if you choose not to learn and or adapt, you will literally watch your competition pass you by. I can't tell you how many times I have seen that happen.

To believe is a choice. Choose to bend and choose to believe in your team. After all, they are only trying to help your company grow.

Refuse to live in fear

Fear is a killer of dreams. It destroys companies from within. You and your team need to choose to not live in fear.

As a leader, you lead by example. You are also, as the leader, going to be hurt, attacked, and challenged. When this occurs, don't let it cause you to live in fear. Let it go and move on.

Remember, if someone is not after your job, you are probably not doing enough to lead! Let objections and challenges push you to be better, stronger, and smarter. That is, after all, what it is supposed to do. Refuse to live in fear. That is how you learn to lead freely.

Ask yourself:

What's the worst that can happen?

You could get fired ... so you would start over. (If you own the company, then the you-are-fired option is not there!)

You could lose your investment ... so you would learn to do it better the next time. You might have to start over with something else you are passionate about. Maybe that is the door you are supposed to walk through anyway!

Be fearless and lead fearlessly. You need it and your team needs it.

At ACS, we spent two years and almost 1.4 million dollars trying to open our own lending company. Many bankers (including a mentor) told me I was crazy. So, we pulled the plug and shut it down.

We then put a plan in place to wait two more years, pay off the debt we accumulated, and open the new company with no outside partners.

Part way into the two-year waiting period, a gentleman walked into our offices and asked if we were looking for a partner for our lending company. Suddenly the wait was over! A few short months later, we were making loans!

Be fearless and do not give up your dreams! Yes, change plans if necessary, but never give up!

PART V

Press On

Leading is not for the weak, but neither is winning. Those who cross the finish line and accomplish their dreams are the ones who chose to press on.

No matter what, press on. You can do it, there is a way. Answers are out there. Just keep going, "falling forward" as some call it, but keep moving toward your goals and dreams.

In the back of this book you will find a list of books I highly recommend to new business owners. One of those is *Failing Forward* by John Maxwell. He gives great insight on what it takes to be successful.

Be one of those few who make it happen!

CHAPTER THIRTEEN

Challenges to Overcome

Every leader has challenges to face. That is because you have chosen *to do* what others have chosen *not to do*. You're going against the flow and your outside-the-box thinking makes you the leader ... and the target.

As a leader, you will face challenges, and though challenges affect everyone differently, it is comforting in a way to know that everyone is dealing with something we must all overcome.

You have your dreams, you know what you are passionate about, so don't let anything or anyone steal that from you. Some believe such a vision gives them license to live by the incredibly short-sighted mantra that the "ends justify the means" for life and business, but that is certainly not the case.

Whatever your challenge, whatever the obstacle in your path, there is a way around it, over it, under it, or through it ... that brings you and your team greater success than ever. Your job is to find out how.

Obstacle #1 – Family expectations

Sometimes people never reach their dreams or fulfill their destiny because of what family members say or believe.

I have witnessed some really innovative thinkers try to lay aside their dreams so they can pick up the family business, though their heart is simply not in it. They have no passion for the work, even if they do have the skill set.

This is a very real challenge, but one that can be addressed with honesty and open dialogue between everyone involved. Find out what the expectations and needs are, and look for solutions.

Sometimes the family opposition is based in the desire for you to be safe and not experience failure. Your family loves you, but they should not try to protect you from using your skills and chasing your dreams.

Discomfort tempts you to return to the status quo.

Their hearts may be in the right place, but they are allowing their fears to rule your life ... and that is never a good thing! You need freedom to take risks and grow.

Whether you are the parent or the child in family challenges, step back and make sure fear is not calling the shots. Sure, we will have setbacks and there will be failures at times, but winners persevere and come back stronger, having learned from those experiences.

Get counsel if you need it, but make the decisions you can be proud of, and let your children chase their dreams as well.

Obstacle #2 – Non-supportive spouse

Many times, spouses don't see the vision of the visionary. They don't understand the hours, the dedication, or the effort it takes to start a business and bring it to a full-blown company.

A spouse may even be jealous that you are living your dream while they may currently be in a dead-end or unfulfilling work environment. A supportive spouse can make or break any business.

Obstacle #3 – No staying power

Another obstacle in the way of your success may be the fact that you lack staying power. By "staying power" I mean your level of commitment to seeing your dream come to pass.

There are always two choices:

> #1 – Choose to stick to it no matter what you face
> #2 – Choose to walk away now

There is absolutely no middle ground. When it comes to staying power, you are either in or you are out.

Those who half-heartedly pursue their dreams could be setting themselves up for a massive disaster. Avoid this by sticking to your dream or deciding to walk away. Whatever your decision, move quickly forward in your decision process.

> No one understands what the entrepreneur goes through on a daily basis like another entrepreneur who has been there.

Sticking to a dream is paramount to any success. If you are not passionate about what you are doing, then you need to find out why you lack the passion that you know you should have.

And if you do choose to walk away, make sure you are not giving up too soon.

Several years ago, I almost left ACS to return to the automotive business. But after much deliberation, which included getting counsel, prayer, and intense mental wrestling, I felt at peace with what I was doing. I had the passion, and I still do, so I decided to stick with it.

Within 60 days of that decision, ACS produced more income in one month than what I would have made in an entire year in the automotive industry. To me, that was a sign I was in the right place.

We cannot give up right before we break through, though we may be tempted to do just that.

If you feel like you lack staying power, no matter the subject and no matter your degree of passion, then you need to address that issue before it comes back to hurt you.

I know a brilliant individual who has some pretty innovative ideas that could be worth a lot of money, because they could help a lot of people … but he has never finished a single one of them. He has no staying power to see his projects through. He is one of the smartest people I have ever met, but he never finishes anything. He has no commitment to seeing anything through to the end.

Oddly, he spends his time tearing other people down and complaining that other people are failing to do their jobs ... all while some pretty innovative new products sit on the shelf in his garage.

Obstacle #4 – Asking for help

Sometimes, the mere act of asking for help is an obstacle that we must overcome. Are we afraid people will think we are not smart enough if we need to ask for help, even for advice?

In the early days of our company, I had no idea what bankers meant when they said, "C and I." There were other banking, business, management, money, and loan terms that I understood, but "C and I" was completely new to me.

Should I ask someone what it means? What will they think of me? We all wonder that in our own situations. But things could only get worse if you don't find an answer.

I went online, and do suggest that as a first option for finding information. If that doesn't work, ask a human.

In the end, I had to ask one of the bank managers for the answer. He explained that "C and I" stood for "Commercial and Industrial" (the section of a bank that handles non-real estate businesses or businesses that are in an owner-occupied real estate building).

He didn't mind explaining it to me. Maybe that helped our relationship grow, because today he is one of our go-to lenders and someone we send a lot of business to.

Mentors and advisors are an important part of the growth of your business. When you have questions, you need people you can turn to and feel confident about the conversations you are having with them.

If you need help, just ask. The act of not getting advice will make you look even dumber, so get on with it and get the help you need.

Obstacle #5 – Refusing to innovate

Nobody ever tells you to your face, "When my business is booming, I'm going to clamp down and refuse to innovate. I'm going to drive my business into the ground."

You just would not do that! But years later, the temptation to stay with the status quo is greater than the desire to change, grow, and innovate … and they drive their business into the ground.

Choose now to always remain in a constant innovative state. Make that your approach, regardless of how "far you have come" or what you have accomplished. That decision will bring greater success for you, your company, and your team than you may ever be able to calculate.

Countless businesses have ceased to exist because the owner or decision makers lived by the philosophy stating, "We have always done it this way and we ain't changing."

History is packed with businesses that failed because they stopped doing what brought them success in the first place.

Along the way, there are warning bells that go off. Perhaps you've heard them coming out of your mouth or the business owner's mouth:

- We aren't changing.
- We've always done it this way.
- We know how to do that.
- We know where the industry is headed.
- We are the experts
- Team members, employees, and certainly customers have nothing to teach us.

Business leaders who think this way are headed for failure. When you as an individual stop learning, you immediately start falling behind. The business world never stands still, which means you are either moving forward, learning, and being innovative ... or you are being passed by someone who is.

Every leader and business must go through changes and evolve. That is the real opportunity to improve and get better, which is what "staying ahead of the curve" is all about.

Just like the warning bells foretelling a bad future, there are other bells that show you are on the right track. Maybe you or the business owner have said:

- What is next for our company?
- How can we better serve our customers?
- What can we do to excel in our industry even more?
- Are there new "gaps" we see that we can fulfill before someone else does?
- What is coming down the road that will make the company more valuable to our clients and our employees?

Years ago, I met the owner of a glass company whose business was thriving. It happened to be a 60-year-old-business! What was his secret? He saw that his industry and model were changing, so he took action. With painstaking effort, he made changes.

Was it easy? No way! Has he faced challenges, even from his banking relationships? You bet! But he made the right call in changing the way his company did business. Today his company is on track for long-term success, and true to form, no doubt he will continue to change and adapt so that he stays ahead!

Obstacle #6 – Lack of capital

Working capital is the money available to start and run your business. Without sufficient working capital, your business cannot survive. Working capital is just that – money you put to work every day. It pays the bills, covers payroll for your employees, and buys the goods that you sell or services you provide.

You need working capital to help generate the cash flow your company needs. Eventually, and as soon as possible, your cash flow will cover your working capital. At that point your business turns a very important corner.

Many years ago, a businessman started a new company in an industry that he had no experience in. After burning through almost $7,000,000 of his own money, he was still a couple years short of turning that corner and generating enough cash flow to stop the financial bleed.

When we met, he was completely out of working capital. We were able to leverage some of his hard assets to get him the working capital he needed to sustain his business until the cash flow improved.

Thankfully, his company stabilized and turned the corner. We were also able to complete an SBA loan to pay off the debt he had accumulated while waiting for the cash flow to catch up. Today, the company's future is bright. But without the working capital, he would not have made it.

Obstacle #7 – Right tools for Business

After ensuring you have sufficient capital, the next technical detail is obtaining the right tools to run your business. This includes such things as phone systems, computers, and the unique equipment your business might need.

Failure to address these issues can destroy your new business before it is even out of the gate! The great news is that there are a lot of small businesses out there that specialize in handling these equipment challenges so you don't have to.

For example, every business needs a payroll system for their employees. When we started, we went with one of the "big boys." The sign up process was pretty smooth, but we quickly learned that the "big boys" did not have time for small business owners. Needless to say, I very quickly changed to a small business that could handle our needs and provide proper customer service.

> One thing that everybody in America agrees on is that attitude is the difference maker in life.
> – *Zig Ziglar*

Funny thing, the "big boy" company bragged they had the best customer service in the industry! Also, they keep sending emails trying to get our business back, but they have never sent someone by our offices to see what our issues were.

Another time, I had an IT specialist who provided us with 10-year-old technology at state-of-the-art pricing. Yes, you can smell the rip off from where you are. The solution to our IT problem eventually came from a small business owner who knew my company and could meet our IT needs. She also happened to be right next door to our office!

Obstacle #8 – Network of Help

You cannot go wrong by cultivating a growing network of people to help you with your business. This can be mentors, other small business owners, training programs, advisors, board members, retired specialists, and even objective family members.

The point is:

> Having a listening ear is sometimes the difference between making a hasty decision and a wise decision.

As you launch and grow your business, keep your networking hat on. Always be looking for sources of good advice and practical help that will enable your business to grow.

The time to be networking is always now, as the need for counsel is always today, right now, this moment! It pays to have a back pocket full of people who can give you good counsel.

Yes, it takes time to build your network, but the secret to doing that is to always keep your eyes and ears open, and that comes from a hunger for growth.

...

As you press on, these types of obstacles will no longer be stumbling blocks. They will transform into stepping stones, stepping stones that move you closer and closer to your intended goals.

That is why you need to overcome every obstacle with your I-will-not-be-denied attitude.

Onwards!

CHAPTER FOURTEEN

Chase Your Dreams

Our days are numbered from the time we are born until the time we die, so why spend your life in a mediocre business or job you have no passion for?

That is a question we all must answer.

Many people have creative ideas they are passionate about, ideas that would be greatly beneficial to countless customers around the world. The challenge is the lack of know-how.

Getting a business started and growing it big are things that many owners have done before. Maybe not with your brilliant idea, but the process of launching and growing a business should never be what blocks you.

At least not any longer!

These details for your business should no longer scare you:

- Starting
- Funding
- Risks
- Partners
- Challenges
- Growth
- Counsel

Nothing has the right or the power to keep you from chasing your dreams. Nothing!

No doubt you have heard the saying:

> "Successful people are successful because successful people are willing to do the things that unsuccessful people are not willing to do!"

Though true at many levels, there is much more involved in being successful. I believe the missing ingredient for many people is the absence or lack of passion.

Passion is the fuel that moves you to do the impossible. Without that fuel, how will you accomplish your dreams and bring your vision to the world?

> Your time is precious, so don't waste it living someone else's life.
> — Steve Jobs

Too many people are stuck in jobs or industries they know are passionless dead ends. That is no way to spend a life!

If you don't believe me, go take a survey of any sales team at an automotive dealership. You are going to find they are a mixed bag of former lawyers, aspiring models, new college graduates, teachers, actors, and more. They are doing what I call "filling time." Few of them are living their dreams, much less working in something they are passionate about.

Rest assured, I am not saying you should immediately quit a job you dislike. Not at all!

What I am saying is that you need to find what moves you, what your passion is, and then set a course to build the opportunity to engage in what that passion is.

You owe it to yourself!

It is never too late

No matter what your circumstances are and no matter where you are in this walk of life, it is never too late to chase your dream or build a great company.

In this land of opportunity, the door is always open.

Choose your dreams

When you look out at the landscape of successful business owners and entrepreneurs, you will find people who work on more than just a job. They work on something they enjoy, love, and are passionate about.

Sometimes you will have to choose your dreams. What happens when you are faced with two great opportunities? Which one do you choose?

Not long ago I had the opportunity to get heavily involved in a very successful business. It was on track to make a lot of money and in a relatively short period of time! It was certainly interesting!

My dilemma was that I already had a business I was passionate about. But I wrestled with the second option. It looked really great on paper.

What would you do? Do you jump in with an amazing company or stay with your passion? Doing both was impossible because both required full-time focus and effort. It was an "all in" type of situation.

Some people argue that money makes up for the lack of passion, but try that on for size after you have done it for many years and tell me if it still fits. I disagree, but your motivation might differ from mine.

My decision was not simple or easy, but I chose to stick with doing what I love and what I am passionate about.

When you run your own business, you are going to have opportunities to start and/or invest in other businesses. What I will tell you is that many businesses have gone under because the owner lost focus. Stay in your lane and stay focused on what you do best – it's what you love and what you know how to do.

Recently, I met a business owner who had been in business for more than 30 years. The company had performed brilliantly for multiple years and made huge net profits year after year. And then … the owner decided to stray from his lane (from the operations he knew and was an expert in).

It cost him all his net worth and a default judgement of over $25,000,000! Fortunately, he was able to buy back his core building and equipment and he managed to keep his core contracts.

The moral of the story:

Stay in your lane!

Whatever you are faced with, your dreams deserve your focused attention and passion. And you deserve to find and do what you are truly passionate about!

I challenge you to uncover what your passion is. Stop and look around. Figure out how to turn that passion into a profitable career that brings financial reward to you and your family. You deserve it!

You already understand completely that there is nobody around who will hand it to you. You have to go out and earn it. You have to make it happen.

This is your opportunity we are talking about ... it is your chance to shine.

It is your time to flourish!

PART VI

Flourish Stories

Finding money to grow and expand. That's what businesses need, but few business owners have a network of advisors and investors who can help.

Part of being successful in business is getting the right funding at the right time. That's what our company does.

Here's to the small business owners who make America what it is today!

CHAPTER FIFTEEN

Automotive Restoration

The Challenge:

Our client is an artist when it comes to restoring classic cars. His work is recognized across the world, not just in the United States. If you ever dreamed of restoring a vehicle from your younger days, this is the guy you would want to do the work. From Mustangs to Corvettes, he is the man.

He had already outgrown the facility where his business was located. In addition, he was leasing from an individual on a month to month basis who kept threatening to rent to someone else and force our client to move. Middle Tennessee has a very tight commercial rental space market, so the threat was very real.

Couple that with the fact that he is rebuilding automobiles and you vastly limit the number of commercial spaces you can rent.

The Solution:

Simply put, our client needed to purchase his own building. In his current marketplace, commercial buildings that pop up for sale are quickly snapped up by investors. He had lost a couple of buildings previously due to not being able to move as fast as he needed too.

In addition, he was asset rich, but cash tight. He and his wife had just purchased a new home and kept their previous home for rental property.

The Result:

The client did a great job of securing a buy/sell agreement on a commercial property, but it came with a caveat. The issue was that the seller demanded he close the deal inside of 30 days. That leaves banks and lenders no time to complete due diligence and necessary third-party reports.

We stepped into negotiations with the seller and showed the seller where the building would not appraise for the sale price. Even though the market is tight and properties are scarce, properties still must appraise for the value close to the sales price. The seller agreed to lower the sales price based on the broker's opinion that the property would come in at the $600,000 value, instead of the initial sale price of $770,000.

We closed a bridge loan for the client that enabled him to meet the closing date demanded by the seller. The cost of the bridge loan was $60,000 with all fees and originations. So, the owner ended up with a bridge loan for $660,000.

Three weeks later the bank took out the bridge loan with a lien on the commercial property and on the residential rental house in the amount of $600,000. We used a second bridge loan for $60,000 to close this loan.

To pay off the remaining $60,000 bridge loan, we facilitated a line of credit for the client and a second line on the commercial property. The client then brought another $7,000 to close the loan.

The client paid $14,000 out of pocket and took out a total loan amount of $674,000 on his commercial building. In 12 months, the client can refinance the bank note and pay off all the lines of credit because the bank will then base their loan proceeds off the appraised value of the property, instead of the sales price.

The client now has his own commercial building to grow and expand his business.

CHAPTER SIXTEEN

Immediate Remodeling

The Challenge:

It's simply not every day that a repeat client calls you and says they need a $6,000,000 line of credit. Our client was finishing a five-star full-service luxury hotel and had run into some cost overruns.

They needed the cash to finish remodeling the entryway for this project and needed it fast!

Their current bank was maxed out on what they could legally loan the clients and so they were handcuffed by the Fed and not able to help the client.

The Solution:

The client needed a line of credit for $6,000,000 and "no" wasn't going to be acceptable. We went to work using the furniture, fixtures, and equipment that they had purchased to go into this five-star luxury hotel as collateral.

They really needed to put the line of credit in place so that they could pay interest only while the new hotel stabilized. Once the hotel reached stabilization, we would refinance the entire hotel project and pay off both the construction loan and the line of credit.

The Result:

We were able to secure a $6,000,000 line of credit utilizing one of our banks through our BancAccess network. The client received an interest-only note and currently the new five-star full-service luxury hotel is open and performing ahead of projections. The refinancing process will soon follow.

CHAPTER SEVENTEEN

Middle Tennessee Hotel

The Challenge:

Our client came to us through a referral from their current bank. The client was maxed out in borrowing ability with this bank and was looking to refinance their existing hotel in middle Tennessee. They also wanted to take some of their equity out of this property to be used on another hotel project they were working on in the Midwest.

The client has a very high net worth and multiple commercial properties ranging from hospitality to assisted living. The client also owns three small community banks. The hotel property is stable and performs much better than the market average.

The client wanted to refinance the hotel property so they could take out $5,000,000 and use it in the Midwest hotel project they were working on.

The Solution:

We secured a regional bank partner to complete this loan. The appraisal came in much lower than expected and after review by the bank, it was determined that the appraiser was light on their evaluation.

The bank had approved a 70% LTV (Loan to Value) for the property and were okay with the client using the cash out of the project to put in their new project. With the lower appraisal numbers, we had to negotiate with the lender on the LTV to get to the numbers that the client was looking for.

The Result:

We secured an 83.3% LTV on the property using the lower than expected appraisal. The client cashed out the $5,000,000 they were needing from this property to put into their new project. The new loan was at a lower rate than the client had been paying. The client's new project is under way and should be stabilized in the next 18-24 months.

As of this writing, we are also working on a $40,000,000 new construction project and a $50,000,000 refinancing project for this client.

CHAPTER EIGHTEEN

Self-Storage Project

The Challenge:

Our client specializes in finding underperforming self-storage facilities and developing them into great performing projects. The client found their latest project in Mississippi, a property owned by an individual who used the units to store his personal items and those of his family and friends. The property was not income producing.

The client entered into a Buy/Sell agreement to purchase the property for $375,000 but had to move quickly to close or lose the opportunity to purchase the property. The client had great credit and a proven track record of success in buying and turning around self-storage properties.

The Solution:

The client had just 2 weeks to close on the property. We facilitated a bridge loan in the amount of $375,000 for a short term while we completed an SBA loan for the property. We closed the bridge loan in a timely fashion, providing the client with control of the property.

We then completed the SBA loan package with the client and have successfully obtained an SBA loan for the property.

The Result:

The client obtained a great property for a great price by moving quickly to close on the property using the bridge loan. The property was appraised for the SBA loan with an "as is" value of $1,050,000 and an "as stabilized" value of $1,600,000.

The SBA loan was completed and closed through one of our national platform lender relationships. The client is now stabilizing the property.

CHAPTER NINETEEN

Tax Trials

The Challenge:

Our client has been in business for over 20 years and has a very successful business. His last year's income was just over $1.8 million after all expenses. The client is debt free.

From 2006 through 2009, our client had a bookkeeper who did a poor job of making sure all taxes were paid. Since 2009, the client has been negotiating and working with a tax specialty firm to resolve their issues with the IRS.

The bookkeeper created a tax liability that grew to $750,000. The client was making too much money to be able to negotiate a settlement with the IRS and the poor record keeping made it impossible to go back and re-state the tax returns for those periods, which, in the opinion of the tax firm, would have resolved the problem or at least reduced the tax liability to our client.

The client's personal credit score was above 760, even though part of the tax lien showed on his personal credit and part showed on his business credit.

The client wanted to resolve the tax lien issue so he could continue to grow his business and eventually purchase his own commercial real estate company.

It should be noted that since 2010, all tax obligations and returns have been filled on time and all tax liability has been paid in full when it was due.

The Solution:

The client had a great A/R and had commercial equipment that put us below a 70% LTV on a $750,000 term note and was seeking a 5-year term on the loan.

Since we began the process, the client continued to pay off an additional $100,000 of the lien, against the advice of his tax firm that is trying to get the IRS to negotiate with them.

Every bank we spoke with regarding this client, loved the client and the business cash flows, but could not get around loaning money to pay off past due tax liens. All the lenders advised us to clear the tax lien and then they would be willing to take out a bridge loan.

The Result:

We secured a loan from a community bank to pay off the tax lien, which enabled our client to get rid of the burden of dealing with the IRS.

The community bank received a long-term and loyal client and the client found a new banking partner.

CHAPTER TWENTY

Getting Out of Your Lane

The Challenge:

We were referred to a client from one of our bank partners who needed a fast solution to save his company. The business had been very successful over the last 30 years and had made tremendous profits during that time. (It is a manufacturing service business with solid contracts with large companies.)

Two years ago, the business owner got outside of his lane and tried to become a developer of a large manufacturing project in Louisiana (his business is in Tennessee). The owner lost millions of dollars on this project and ended up having to have his company file for bankruptcy protection.

The client had a $29,000,000 default judgement against him and his wife personally and had the business in a bankruptcy liquidation.

The Solution:

Fortunately, the business owner had a great attorney who structured a non-revocable family trust for the business owner. The business owner saved his existing business contracts and began doing business under the new company that was owned by the trust.

This kept the cash flow going to sustain the business's normal operations and cash flows and met the requirements for the company to be able to service the ongoing contracts with its clients.

We then had to find a way to buy back one of the buildings the company had previously owned and see if we could get the bankruptcy court to sell the equipment needed to stay in business to the new company.

Finding a financing solution we could get the courts to agree with was a major concern.

The Result:

The attorney worked with the court and was able to allow the business owner to purchase one of the buildings and some of the essential equipment that was needed to sustain operations.

We provided a bridge loan to allow the purchases to be completed and keep the new company up and running. This saved 15 jobs in a small rural area of Tennessee. The client is performing as he did prior to the bankruptcy and this will allow the company to return to profitability.

CHAPTER TWENTY-ONE

Collision Center Magic

The Challenge:

A client was referred to ACS from a business broker who was trying to get a deal closed for a new startup company. Unfortunately, they had waited too long to get the financing completed in a normal time frame using an SBA 7A loan.

Most people will tell you closing a typical SBA loan takes four to six months. This client had less than 90 days remaining to close this transaction.

When you have a client who is trying to fulfill their dreams of owning their own business, it makes you want to work that much harder to help!

The prospective business owners had been in the collision center business (auto repair) all their adult lives. They now wanted to work for themselves. They had the blessing of insurance companies who had gotten to know them and raved about their work. They just needed to open their own business.

We also had a seller, a large corporation, that was leaving this city.

The Solution:

When you are dealing with commercial real estate financing and part of that property has been a collision center, there are going to have to be environmental inspections to make sure there are no chemicals that have seeped into the ground. Couple that with the normal needs of appraisals and you can quickly see why this loan would typically take at least four months to close.

The client had 20% down to complete the financing, but the SBA was going to require an additional 5% down to make this deal work.

The owners were still working their previous jobs everyday while we worked to get the financing they needed in place. Luckily, one of the wives of the clients was able to work with us daily so we could expedite the closing.

We also had the issue of putting together the additional 5% that was needed for the down payment on the SBA loan.

The Solution:

We completed the financing for this project in 59 days from start to finish. We worked diligently with one of our best SBA lending partners and they worked with the same urgency as we did to close this loan.

We made an introduction between the clients and a business investor who put the additional 5% into the deal that was needed for the SBA 7A loan.

This deal could not have closed this quickly if not for the client's wife helping us to get the documentation and items required for the loan approval, appraisal, environmental reports, and the closing.

Our team is outstanding at SBA lending, but the client must be willing to work diligently to move any SBA deal from start to finish in just 59 days, let alone one with real estate and environmental inspections needed!

The Result:

Closing the deal in less than 60 days from the time the client engaged us until we closed the SBA 7A loan with our lending partner was a fast-paced project! But it paid off.

The clients were able to leave their regular jobs and opened their new collision center immediately. Their business is now up, running, and growing daily. What they have always been known for in the past lives on today in the form of their new business!

CHAPTER TWENTY-TWO

Closing Fast & Furious

The Challenge:

On Valentine's Day, I happened to be out on a date with my wife, Tabitha, and we were sitting at one of my favorite places to eat (Connors, in Brentwood, TN) and my phone started ringing over and over.

Earlier that day I had received a call from a banker who referred a client to us who needed immediate funding on a commercial real estate project or he was going to lose the property. The client had already received one extension on the property, when the seller realized the true value of the property.

The sale price was $1,350,000, but with the new zoning on the property, it was worth north of $2,000,000. The seller wanted out of the contract and the buyer needed to close in 7 days or lose the property.

I finally took the call with the client and went through the list of what I would need to close his deal through a bridge loan in a mere seven days.

Then I reached out to several investor/lenders we have worked with in the past (my wife was very patient!). I put most of the funds together to close the deal within an hour and finished the raising of the funds the next morning.

The Solution:

To facilitate such a fast closing is never easy. What helped us was that one of the investor/lenders was very familiar with the property and assured me the value was there.

The client said he only needed the funds for six months and he was willing to sign a deed in lieu, which meant that if he didn't pay off the loan when it was due, the investor/lenders would own the property and be able to then sell it for the higher value.

The Result:

We closed the loan in five days and the client secured the property from a reluctant seller. The client then used the next six months to secure his next phase of funding and paid off the bridge loan.

What the property will look like when it's completed is still up in the air, but the client now controls his own destiny with the help of our bridge lending program.

CHAPTER TWENTY-THREE

A Monster Line of Credit

The Challenge:

When one of the wealthiest families in America calls you to get a line of credit, you must figure out how to make that deal happen! Our client called us and was looking for a $20,000,000 line of credit for business growth and expansion and they did not want to use their own funds.

There are many wealthy investors and families who do not use family funds when borrowed money is available. This was the case with this client. The problem was the limited real estate involved with these operations and the fact that this was a relatively new line of business for the group.

With not very much historical data to go from, we had to lean on the net worth of the client and find a bank that could understand what we were trying to accomplish.

The Solution:

Thankfully, at ACS we have a community bank network that is usually aggressive on deals that fit their lending niche. We went to work underwriting this deal for our client and presented a lending opportunity to our BancAccess network that proved to be a great opportunity.

Community banks like commercial loans that fund and grow their market share. One bank partner was willing to take this on and moved toward closing this rather large line of credit.

The Result:

Without us bringing this client to the bank, they would have never had access to this client, and without us bringing the client to the bank, the client would have never suspected that this community bank could provide such a large line of credit. When this happens, everybody wins!

CHAPTER TWENTY-FOUR

Financing Dreams & Dirt

The Challenge:

A business broker came to us for help. He was trying to help a company finance a piece of land to build an independent living center, which usually consists of townhomes, condos, or single-family residences for a community with age restrictions.

The company had bought the raw land for a fair price, but they needed the funding to get the property ready for development. The plans needed to be approved by the county and initial studies of the dirt had to be performed to determine the most profitable use for the land.

None of these activities are free, so the client needed to secure a loan against the land they had purchased (with cash) to pay for these expenses.

The Solution:

The hardest loan to get approved in commercial lending is raw land. The value of raw land is so speculative that it can be hard to get an accurate appraisal of what the land is worth.

When you couple that with the fact that land is valued by what it's used for, it makes financing raw land very difficult.

Our client owned an adjoining piece of land and their master plan included joining the two pieces of land together to create an assisted living facility and a new independent living center.

The problem with their loan request was that banks do not typically lend money against raw land, and especially not raw land that has yet to go through any of the land development requirements. The client was also low on cash because of their ongoing efforts to get the assisted living facility up and running.

The Result:

We secured the client a bridge loan so they could complete the initial phases of the land development. This allowed the client to get the plans approved by local zoning authorities and have the development of the independent living center design completed and approved.

After completing this phase of the development of the project, the client was free to pursue construction financing for the independent living center.

Conclusion

There is no greater responsibility than to family. A parent's responsibility is to provide a feeling of safety where their children can grow, prosper, and learn to become young adults. They in turn will teach their own families how to do the same.

The similarities between parents and small business owner are plain. My number one responsibility in our company is to make sure that my family members – *the team around me* – grow and prosper, and in some cases become young entrepreneurs themselves.

To do that, I am tasked with providing them with a secure feeling that our company will make it, that payroll is not a problem, and that I have the financial success of our company and their future as my number one priority.

Some days those priorities are easier to meet than others. I always try to come into our offices with a smile on my face, a positive attitude, and a can-do spirit. Fortunately for me, we have had more great days than bad days and we have simply been blessed.

I have tried to do what is right by my team first and to put myself in their shoes to see how I would feel about some of the decisions I have made. I have not always been successful, such as at times hiring the wrong people to grow our company or parting with team members who actually needed me to be flexible and creative in placing them in a different position.

Every chapter in this book is based on experiences I have had in building ACS and our affiliate companies. If you are a seasoned business owner and you believe I have missed an important chapter, then it is very likely I have simply not experienced that situation in our company yet!

A few final thoughts:

You are the creative thinker in your company, but that does not mean those around you don't have great insight or ideas to grow and expand your company. I started ACS out of the basement of my home here in Franklin, Tennessee and Ken Collins was in Conroe, Texas. I can tell you today that without Ken to bounce ideas off and to get his opinions, ACS would not have made it.

Now that Ken is somewhat retired, I cannot imagine running our company without the assistance of my oldest son, Jeff or without our Senior Credit Officer, Micah Seadorf. I have told Micah on many occasions that if she ever leaves, I just need to know where to show up because I am not doing this without her. I hope my actions let her know how important she is to me. Jeff has gained more lending knowledge than I ever had and is paramount to the success of all our companies. His thought process and drive to succeed are unmatched and I am fortunate that he loves what we do as much as I do.

My point is that great people are hard to find, and when you do find them, do all you can to hold on to them!

You are critically vital to your company, so learn to take care of yourself. I was at lunch not long ago with my wife and another couple we recently met. The gentleman told us how lucky he was to have always loved what he did for a living. That is truly my story.

As I have said earlier, I am blessed to love what I do and it doesn't feel like work. That can be great at times but can also cause issues when I fail to turn things off. We all need our downtime and we need the time to spend with family and friends. Knowing when to shut it down for a while has certainly been a struggle for me.

> With business, it's how you start *and* how you finish that matters.

If you don't learn to shut it down and take care of yourself with rest, relaxation and a recharging period, you will quickly burn out and not be an effective owner of your company. Your health matters, so be sure you rest. This will in turn make your thought process more focused and provide you with new creative thinking to continue to grow, expand, and evolve your business model. Take care of yourself. You are an important asset to your company!

Lastly, if you think you know it all or that you have all the answers, you don't. Find yourself a great business coach and then listen to their advice. I am not saying do everything they tell you to do, but do listen to their thoughts and advice they have to offer. Then when you have examined all the facts, make a great decision and move on.

Many owners get caught in one of two phases:

> **Phase #1:** They know it all and refuse anyone's help.

> **Phase #2:** They are unsure of the direction to go, can't make decisions and freeze in place.

As a small business owner, you are a leader in your community. Whether you choose to be or not, people are watching your actions, your decision making, and how your company performs. (Some people are even secretly hoping you will fail. They are actually afraid to do what you have done and would rather you fail so you come back to their level.)

If you own your own business, you are going to have setbacks and some failures. Simply refuse to quit, learn from your mistakes, and FLOURISH!

Recommended Reading

Failing Forward, John C Maxwell

Make Your Bed, William H. McRaven

See You at the Top, Zig Ziglar

Secrets of Closing the Sale, Zig Ziglar

You Win in the Locker Room First, John Gordon and Mike Smith

4th and Goal Every Day, Phil Savage

Books by John C. Maxwell:
- *Talent is Never Enough*
- *Developing the Leader Within You*
- *The Difference Maker*
- *The 15 Invaluable Laws of Growth*

Advanced Reading Recommendations

Makers and Takers, Rana Foroohar

Good to Great, Jim Collins

Great by Choice, Jim Collins and Morten T. Hansen

What it Takes, by Stephen Schwarzman

How the Mighty Fall, Jim Collins

The Creature from Jekyll Island, G. Edward Griffin

Reference books kept in my office:

- Dictionary of Finance and Investment Terms, John Downes and Jordan Elliot Goodman
- Dictionary of Business and Economics Terms, Jack P. Friedman
- *How Money Works*, DK

The Funding
Money Flow

Option #1:

A business owner needs money, but doesn't know who to talk to or how to request it. The usual result is:

- confusion
- frustration
- no funding

Option #2:

At ACS, we know who to talk to and how to request the funding. The usual result is:

- clear communication
- efficiency
- quick funding

If you are a new business or an existing business needing extra funds to expand your operations:

- call us directly at 615-538-7814
- or visit us at ACStn.net